M000104657

Made in United States
North Haven, CT
17 June 2022

20347982R00065